Penny Stocks

A Complete Guide to Buy And Trade Penny Stocks

Alvin Williams

The information in the following pages is broadly considered to be a truthful and accurate account of facts, and as such any inattention, use or misuse of the information in question by the reader will render any resulting actions solely under their purview. There are no scenarios in which the publisher or the original author of this work can be in any fashion deemed liable for any hardship or damages that may befall them after undertaking information described herein.

Additionally, the information found on the following pages is intended for informational purposes only and should thus be considered, universal. As befitting its nature, the information presented is without assurance regarding its continued validity or interim quality. Trademarks that mentioned are done without written consent and can in no way be considered an endorsement from the trademark holder.

TABLE OF CONTENTS

A Complete Guide to Buy And Trade Penny Stocks

How To Start Trading Penny Stocks

Introduction

Congratulations on downloading your personal copy of *Penny Stocks: A Complete Guide to Buy And Trade Penny Stocks.* Thank you for doing so.

In this guidebook, we are going to spend some time learning about penny stocks and why they are one of the best options to consider when it is time to get into the world of investing. While there are many options that come from working inside the world of investing, penny stocks can be an interesting choice that will bring in a lot of profit. This guidebook is going to go over them in more detail so that you can learn how to use this investing tool.

First we will start with some of the basics of penny stocks and how they are different from the other stocks that you can choose from and we will discuss the two main options with penny stocks; namely the Pink Sheets and the Over-the-Counter Bulletins. Once we have had a chance for you to learn about these basics, it is time to get into the world of penny stock investing. We will talk about how to get into the game and find a good broker before moving in to some of the top strategies that you can use to put your money to work and see the penny stocks work for you. We will then end the guidebook with some basic tips that can help you to really see results even as a beginner.

Working in penny stocks is a great way to open up your portfolio so that your money can grow more than ever before, but it does take some time and effort in order to learn this method and get it to work well for you. This guidebook is going to give you the tips that you need in order to get started making a good income with penny stocks.

There are plenty of books on this subject on the market, thanks again for choosing this one! Every effort was made to ensure it is full of as much useful information as possible. Please enjoy!

Chapter 1:

What is Penny Stock Investing?

Investing is something that many people are interested in. They want to see how much their money can grow for them and some even want to see if they can make this a full time income rather than working their regular jobs. There is a variety of investments that you are able to make. Some people keep it safe and place their money in a savings account while others go with a retirement plan. Some will go with real estate and choose one of those options when the market is good and others like to start their own business, get into the stock market, or invest in a friend who is doing something new. The options can be endless when it comes to starting a new investment, and picking out the right one for you can be the hardest part of getting started.

One investment type that you may wan to try is the penny stock. This is a type of stock that starts out really low, at no more than $1 for each of the shares. According to the Securities and Exchange Commission in the United States, a penny stock is one that will trade at no more than $5 a share, but most of them will be less than that.

A penny stock can bring about a huge profit to those who know how to use it, but it is not a popular option as it works off the regular stock market and it often used when a company is really desperate for some money. There is the potential for large losses, even if you make the purchase at a small rate, but if you are able to read the market, there is the potential to see a great deal and make a good profit in the process.

One of the best ways to ensure that you aren't taking a big loss on these stocks is to be careful who you purchase from. There are some unscrupulous people who will make a big purchase of penny stocks in order to help raise the price. They will use fake press releases, websites, stock message boards and more to talk up the penny stock so more people will make a purchase and then the price goes up even more. Then they sell the stocks at the inflated price, making themselves a lot of money while everyone else will not be able to find any buyers and will either have to hold onto the stock or sell it at a loss.

The good news is that the penny stock does need to meet some standards in order to prevent the process above, which is known as pump and dump. Inside the United States, these stocks need to have a price, market capitalization, and a minimum shareholder equity. Remember that even if the stock you are looking at is below $5, it will not be a penny stock unless it is traded off of the stock exchange.

The good about penny stocks

We spent a little time talking about some of the things that you will need to avoid when using penny stocks and looking to invest in these opportunities. If you are careful about watching the market and seeing what is going on before you make a purchase, you should be able to figure out when a pump and dump scheme is going on. If something looks like it is rising in price too quickly, you see that there was only one buyer of a large amount of penny stocks with just one company, or you feel like this person is really trying to pressure someone into making a purchase that doesn't look like the best, it is a good idea to go with a different option for the penny stocks.

The good news is that you are able to do well in penny stocks, you just have to keep your head and make sure that you aren't trying to rush into something that doesn't make sense or that has a lot of red flags all over it. One of the best ways to get the most out of your penny stocks is to learn how to do your research before making any purchases.

There are many things that you will be able to research about a penny stock before you get started. For example, start by looking at the corporate website for the company you want to work with. this provides you a good idea about the company because a lot of information can be there. You should then look at the balance sheet of the company to see how many debts the company is dealing with; if there are too many debts, the company may be trying to sell the penny stocks to get out of debt, but if they haven't learned how to control that debt, throwing more money over to them will not help. You want to pick penny stocks out from companies that are profitable or the ones who are able to properly reduce their losses and will not take on large amounts of debt to keep running.

Penny stocks can be a great form of investing if you are looking to get started with an option or you want to expand out your portfolio out to make your money work a little harder. We are going to take a look at more parts about penny stocks and how you will be able to make them go to work for you.

Chapter 2:

What are Pink Sheets?

So before we get into some of the basics of trading in penny stocks, we need to take some time to understand the different methods that companies can list themselves in this kind of market. Remember that while there are rules for penny stocks, they are not considered part of the stock market so working with them is going to be a bit different than what you are used to. Here we are going to talk about how a company is able to list in Pink Sheets and what this means for you the investor.

Listing in Pink Sheets

For a company to get started with penny stocks, they will first need to file the Form 211 in order to be listed in Pink Sheets. This is a privately held corporation, compared to the other option (which we will talk about later) over-the-counter Bulletin Board, which is a service that is owned by the

NASDAQ. There are many companies that use Pink Sheets to work with and when they fill out the Form 211, they will need to submit it over to the OTC Compliance Unit. The market maker is going to process the listing for the company. The broker and dealer will be able to quote a price for this company, as long as the company is pretty transparent. However, there are some companies that won't commit to this transparency because they won't submit their current information on business financials.

For the companies that are listed using the Pink Sheets, you will find that they are a small and a thin trader. This company will not have to work with the SEC during trading time and they don't have to file their periodic reports. Now some of them will do this filing in order to show what they are doing and to help the investor feel more comfortable with working with them, but this is not a requirement. In many cases, it can be difficult to get information in order to understand companies that are on the Pink Sheets because you just don't have the information that is needed to get started.

The benefits of trading Pink Sheets

Despite the fact that the companies who use Pink Sheets are not required to be transparent or file periodic updates, an investor is usually going to find some pretty good options to trade in penny stocks with these Pink Sheets. You have the possibility of getting a high return because these are the stocks that are volatile. There are also some companies that are in this group that used to be strong, but for some reason or another had to leave the major exchanges because of a strict requirement they no longer met. They may still be good companies to trade with and you could make some good profits from it.

It is also possible to find obscure companies to trade with in order to help that company grow before they move over to one of the major exchanges. You would be able to invest with these companies early on and this could give you a huge reward later as they start to grow and move over to the stock exchange.

In addition, the Pink Sheets system has a tier system that helps you to differentiate between the companies that are there. This helps you to figure out which stocks are higher risk and which ones are lower risk based on the classifications that are set. You are able to pick whichever risk setting that you are happy and comfortable with, but as a beginner, it is nice to know which ones fall into each category to help you make a decision.

If you want to use the Pink Sheets as part of your trading, you need to make sure that you really do your research. Pink Sheets is not going to provide you with much information about the companies you are trading with and if you just randomly pick a company, you are increasing your risk and making it likely that you will lose all of your money.

The classifications system

As mentioned before, the Pink Sheets system has a classification for each of the companies that trade using it. This makes it easier to determine whether a company is high risk or low risk and you can make your decisions based on this. Some of the tiers that are found inside of the classification system include:

Trusted tier

Inside of the trusted tier in Pink Sheets, you will find the international as well as American companies that are considered trustworthy and investor friendly. The companies that are from other countries are going to be on the international exchange, but they can still fit into this trusted tier. The companies that are in this tier have not met the requirements to be on the regular stock exchange, but this is usually because of one or two small things since the stock exchange is so strict.

However, even though these companies were not able to get onto the stock exchange, they were able to pass an independent audit. This list sometimes does include companies in American that pass the standards needed for NASDAQ but they aren't submitting SEC reports and so they would be moved over to Pink Sheets instead.

Transparent Tier

This is a tier that will send in SEC reports and

sometimes will also include those that are in Over-the-Counter Bulletin Boards. These are highly trusted companies because you will be able to see some of their financial reports as well as other information that is required for them to be good with the SEC. You will be able to do your research on these companies because it is provided to you and can save a lot of guesswork and hassle when choosing the penny stocks you want to work with.

Distressed Tier

Companies that are inside of this tier of Pink Sheets are ones that provide limited information for the investor to look at and often they are not following the guidelines that are set out by Pink Sheets. These companies may not even send out updated information to the SEC like they should, but some them will work with the OTC disclosures. Not all of these are bad to work with, but sometimes you need to be wary because they aren't sending out the right information and some of them have been bankrupt.

Dark Tier

This is the tier that you will really need to watch out for because it could cause some issues. Companies that are inside of this particular tier aren't sending in any information about their business. They aren't filing information with either the SEC or the OTC Disclosure service and they haven't done so over at least the last six months, making it really hard for the investor to have any idea how this stock is doing. There are some companies that get into this tier that are also failing with transparency in the market or they don't have a market marker.

Toxic Tier

As a new investor, or any investor for that matter, it is best to stay out of the toxic tier. Companies that are in this tier will often rely on marketing strategies that are fraudulent such as using promotions that are questionable or sending out a lot of spam to name a few. These can also include some companies that are subjected to large corporate events that disrupt them or they may have a suspension by the government. In some cases, these will not actually have their own business operations and can be really dangerous to send your money to.

Taking a look at these different types of tiers inside this system can help you to make a more informed choice when it comes to work in the Pink Sheets. You will be able to see these rankings with any of the companies that you choose to go with and if you pick the one with the highest reputation, it becomes easier to get good returns on investments.

How to make decisions in Pink Sheets

So now that we know a bit more about Pink Sheets and how they work, it is time to learn how to do the trading decisions. When picking out a penny stock that is inside of Pink Sheets, you are going to be limited on information and technical analysis of most of the companies. There are also some issues on occasion because there isn't a central exchange that you can use to buy and trade these stocks. This is why it is best to start out with a broker and dealer who will be able to walk you through this process.

As the investor, you will need to do a fundamental

analysis of any company that you want to invest in, even if they are not sending the information your way. You can look at the different companies and their past history and you can look to see if there are some hidden gems that other people will miss out on right now, but which will make the stock better later on. With some good research, you will quickly be able to narrow down the choices that you want to use.

Working with Pink Sheets can be one way to get started on penny stocks, but you do need to be careful. Some of the companies are great and will provide you with information to pick them; many of these are working to get to the stock exchange, but for some small reason or another, they are not quite there yet and these are pretty safe options to go with. But there are also companies on the Pink Sheets that won't provide any information, and some that are even fraudulent, so you need to be careful about the companies that you invest in to help keep your portfolio strong and growing.

Investing with OTC Bulletin Boards

Another option that you can choose to invest for your penny stocks is the Over-the-Counter Bulletin Boards, or the OTC Boards. This one, at least inside of the United States, is operated through the Financial Industry Regulatory Authority and it will hold many of the stocks and securities that are not found on the NASDAQ or other stock exchanges. You will need to work with brokers and dealers in order to order the penny stocks since this is not an electronic method, and it can be pretty secure to work with.

This type of penny stock is usually seen as a little more secure because they are required to send in financial information and to be transparent. It is regulated a bit more and often the companies that are on this one will be here because they didn't meet some small requirement to be on the exchange. All of the companies that are listed on these bulletin boards will need to report their information to the SEC, but they don't have to include as much information as they would on the stock exchange and they can leave our information on their market capitalization, minimum share price, governance, and more.

These are usually seen as a bit more secure because of the fact that these companies have to send in information and report to the SEC while the companies on the Pink Sheets could do this reporting, but they didn't have to. Many beginners in penny stocks will choose to go with this option because it allows them to learn a bit more about the company that they want to invest in, making it easier to pick a smart investment on their end of things.

Both the OTC Bulletin Boards and the Pink Slips can be great places to start in order to find the penny stock that you want to work with. Some of the options can be a bit risky, but as a good investor, it is up to you to step in and do the research to find this information out. You are going to find risky investments no matter where you are, whether on or off the stock market or in other forms of investing, but you need to find the one that works the best for you and has the right risk to reward ratio that you are comfortable with. Both of these trading methods have their own systems to help you to make these decisions and if you are working with a broker and a dealer, you should have the support that you need to make the right decisions.

Chapter 3:

Getting Started with the Penny Stocks

Now that you know a bit more about working with penny stocks, it is time to work on putting some money into the stock that you would like to use and making sure that you get the right stock that will help you to make the money that you would like from this option. This chapter is going to help you learn how to get started with the penny stocks so that you can see the profits that you want in no time.

Opening your account

So the first step for you to do when starting on penny stocks is to pick out and open up a trading account. As an investor, you need to consider how easy the account is to work with. You should think about how easy it is to transfer the accounts too and from the account, the customer service with the account, and any fees that are associated with opening and running the account. There are times when a broker will choose a fixed rate for a smaller amount of shares but this rate can increase when you trade on more shares; depending on the type of trading that you do, this could make a big difference in the profit that you make.

The nice thing about working on a commission per share idea is that it works well for investors who want to get into penny stocks but who don't have a lot of extra money for this. As the investor, you will need to shop around in order to find the best broker and the best trading account to help open up your options and maximize your profits so take the time to look at and talk to a few different companies to determine which one is the best for you to open up.

Picking out your penny stocks

When you are ready to find the penny stocks and make a decision, you will need to choose which one you want to use from the Over-the-Counter Bulletin Board or from the Pink Sheets. You should be able to receive a list of the stocks that are available for you to use and you can do your research and pick the ones that you would like. Some brokers are able to provide you some screening tools so that you are better able to pick out the stock for your risk tolerance and your investing strategy.

Since penny stocks are a very volatile investment, it is possible to make a lot of money from your investment, but it is also possible to lose a lot of money in the process as well. This means that you need to never rush into the trades and you need to think some of them through.

There aren't a lot of people who invest in penny stocks, including money managers, index funds, and various mutual funds, which is one of the reasons that the penny stock market is going to be so volatile. Since here aren't many investors that go with this option, you may have times that there are liquidity problems. You may not be able to share some of the stocks that you own because there just aren't buyers available who would take the stock at all, much less at the price that you would like. You may have to take a big loss and really sell them at a low price in order to earn any money back, but it may be at a loss. But there is also a possibility that these stocks will go the other way and you are able to sell them at a much higher value than you purchased them. But it is the job of the investor to decide which way this is going to go before making a purchase of a penny stock.

Choosing a broker

A broker is an important person who will help you to get started on the penny stocks. A broker is going to be in charge of providing you with the platform that you need in order to work on your trades. They can work with you to provide some recommendations for what stocks to purchase, as well as providing marketing and sales services for all stakeholders. They will have a lot of tools and advice that you would be able to use when you get started. Every broker that you work with will have different services and tools that you can utilize, so this should go into consideration when it comes to picking out the broker you want to work with.

Many of the brokers you want to consider will have a good presence online and some will offer trading platforms that work on mobile devices. You can also work with some that offer bank accounts or nostro for trading these shares. No matter what method you are using for your trading and which one you think is best, it is important that you choose a broker who is able to provide you with reliable and instant money transfers so that you are able to complete your trades in the right time.

If your broker is slow at doing these transfers for you, you may end up losing out on a lot of money because you pay more than expected for the stock or they aren't quick enough at getting you out of the game so be careful with this when working with them.

Some other things that you should consider when picking out a broker is the fees and charges they are going to give to you. All brokers are going to want some fees to help pay them for doing their job, but learn right from the beginning how much they are going to charge you and what it all depends on (such as if they charge one rate for a small amount of trades and then another rate for many trades). Always look at the terms and conditions on the website of your broker to see if you agree with everything that the broker will do for you as well as your own responsibilities.

Rules to ensure you make a profit when trading penny stocks

While there is going to be some risk when you go into penny stocks, there are a few rules that you will be able to follow to make it easier to make some money with penny stocks. Some of the rules that are best for your trading include:

- The investor needs to have a plan in place right from the start that helps them to know their entering and exiting strategy. This helps to keep some of the emotions out of the game.

- The investor needs to know when it is time to exit. You should cut your losses when the market starts to become unpredictable so that you don't lose more money.

- The investor needs to make sure that the reward is larger than the risk. You never should enter into a trade that seems as a sure loss.

- The investor must have a good scheme for managing their money. They must always keep this in mind when picking out a penny stock.

- The investor should never trade using their emotions. This is sure to lead to a big loss that will get worse when the emotions come into play. They must have discipline in the emotional times and learn how to follow their plan of investment all the time.

- The investor should avoid trading during the first hour of the day. There are many older investors who use this time to work on selling shares to beginners and they know that the price is going to go down. They hope to make a profit during this time before the stock goes down. So wait a few hours and then do your trading.

- The investor should never invest more money than they are able to lose. This is a really risky option for investing and it is speculative. It is possible to earn a good profit if you are smart about your investments, but never get so into the game that you invest more than you have to lose.

Learning to minimize your risks

When it comes to penny stocks, it is important to realize that this is a really risky way to invest your money. You are not working with items that are on the stock exchange and sometimes getting the information that you need in order to make informed decisions can be almost impossible to do. While you can make a lot of money with penny stocks, it is also possible to lose a lot of money in the process as well.

Luckily, there are some things that you are able to do in order to severely minimize your risk with penny stocks. There are a few things that you must watch out for because these help to show that a stock is too risky to work with. for example, if you notice that a company has a small operation and only a modest market capitalization, it is one of the riskier investments. Another thing to watch out for is stocks that sell too low. These stocks are going to trade at lower than $1 a share because these need to have a lot of caution so that the amount doesn't go lower.

Some people think that all big companies started out with penny stocks and this is why they choose to go into this kind of investment. There are a few that do start out as penny stocks to get the funds that they need before moving into the stock market, but this is abnormal and most do not work this way.

So why are some companies interested in offering these penny stocks when there are options. Some companies will go with the penny stock when they want to pay for something expensive in the company or when they are looking to expand. The company can offer the penny stocks in order to distribute some of its profits and make changes to its tax structure each year. Some brokerage firms will convince companies to offer up these stocks because the brokers want to earn some money from investors. Some companies will even offer these penny stocks if it determines that they are not going to grow any more in the future and they would like to place the ownership on the investors.

This is why you need to be careful about the penny stocks that you get into. Some are just looking for some help to expand and they will be reputable options that you can make some money on if you are careful and do your research. But others are just trying to offload some of their responsibilities or they want to get a tax break, rather than help you out, and you could end up losing a lot of money. When you go into the penny stock, a good way to think about it is that these companies don't really care about the investor. If you have this wary thought in your head when investing, you are more likely to pick out a stock that benefits you the most.

Scams and penny stocks

Scams are pretty prevalent inside of penny stocks because they are not part of the normal stock exchange so the rules are pretty lack on them. Many of the companies don't even follow the SEC rules or file with them well so getting information that you need can be difficult. It is easy for scams to arise in this situation.

As the investor, you need to be careful with your money and watch out for these scams. There are many good companies you can trade with and make some good money on, but there are also lots of bad brokers who will try to just take your money, bad companies that want to make money quick, and even other investors who will start buzz to bring up their own stocks and earn higher than they paid for a bad stock. You need to be independent and learn to think on your own so that you can get the best return on investment and not get taken in by one of the scams.

Getting started on penny stocks is pretty easy as long as you learn which companies to trust, pick out a good trading account, and find a broker who will not charge you too many fees to work with. Add in some good research and one of the trading strategies that we will talk about below, and you are all set to making some great money with penny stocks.

Some misconception about the penny stocks

It is common for people who want to make money

off these penny stocks to start spreading some rumors and misinformation about how penny stocks will work. It is likely that you have heard at some point that penny stocks where the way that many popular stocks on the market got started out. These rumors are started in order to get new investors to purchase stocks that they wouldn't otherwise at a higher price because they want to be in on the ground floor of a company that is going to go big. However, as a diligent investor, you will find out that this is not true and the only reason that some of these companies had stocks that were worth less money is because they split up their stocks, not because they started out as penny stocks.

Some people also assume that because a company is in penny stocks, it is not safe to trade on at all. This is true in some cases; there are some companies who just want to make money quickly and then leave you with something that is worthless, but there are also some companies that are using this as a way to help them out. The regulations for getting on the stock market are pretty strict and some companies are really great, but miss out by a little bit for getting onto the stock market. They may start out on the penny stock while they work on making it to the stock market, but there is nothing fundamentally wrong with them. These are the companies that you will want to work with because they can make the best return on investment.

It is never a good idea to go into penny stocks thinking that it is easy. There are many brokers and others who are in this business who will try to tell you all their success stories and try to convince you that anyone is able to get into penny stocks and make a fortune. These people are usually trying to get you to buy into something so that they can make more money as well. Penny stocks are hard work and you need to keep at them and really do your research, not just listen to what another investor or a broker are telling you.

There are a lot of misconceptions that are out there about penny stocks. Some of them may be a little bit true, but many of them are just because of the buzz that is around the penny stocks to get you to purchase them or they are from people who just don't understand how the market works. Before you invest your hard earned money, make sure to take a step back and really understand how these kinds of stocks work so that you can make the best decisions possible.

Chapter 4:

Strategies in Penny Stocks

Now that we have spent some time talking about penny stocks and how to get started on them and we did all the research, it is time to work on dealing with the penny stocks. If the stock is a good one (which you should be able to determine from the research that you did before) it is time to pick out the strategy that you are going to use in order to get started. Keep in mind that if you are going with a popular stock, the price is going to be high to start with and it can be hard to get started.

Before we look at some of the strategies that you are able to use with penny stocks, we need to remember that it is not a good idea to chase a stock. Chasing means that you will raise your buying price quickly because you are desperate to get the shares instead of someone else. This is a really bad thing to work with because your emotions are going to start running and you will often spend a lot more on the stock (and sometimes it will be a bad stock) than it is worth. Eventually the buyers who chased the stock will find that the value of the stocks will go down and the price will go the same way, making it hard to sell them at all, even for a loss.

One thing that you should remember is that it is important to pick out a strategy that you want to work with and then stick with it. Most of the strategies that are listed below, as well as some of the others that you may find or hear about in your work, are going to help you to make a good return on investment if you learn how to use them properly and you don't skip from one strategy to another.

Some beginners find that when they make a trade and it doesn't work while using one strategy, they will try to move over to another strategy and get this one to give them some of the results that they need. They assume that there was something wrong with that initial strategy and that they just need to try something else. The problem comes when they do this over and over again, switching strategies each time that something goes wrong.

This is an example of letting the emotions get in the way of what you want to do. If you are always switching out the strategy that you want to use, you are never really learning how to use one of them and your whole plan is going to become a mess. You need to pick one and really get to know it, understanding how it works from all angles and in all situations, in order to get the best results with your trading. Over time you may find that it is better to get rid of one strategy and change it to another because the one isn't working or you find one will work better with your style, but it is never a good idea to skip around on the strategies that you are using all the time because it is just going to confuse you and makes it hard to ever see the success that you want with penny stocks.

The good news is that when you pick a strategy to work with inside of penny stocks, you are able to avoid the issues with chasing or some of the other issues that can come up when using penny stocks and trying to make a purchase. There are many strategies that you are able to pick from so you don't have to feel that you are only going to be able to use one and not feel comfortable with it. Some of the trading strategies that you may want to consider when working with penny stocks include:

Day Trading

When it comes to working with day trading, the investor is going to buy and then also sell their security in just one day, sometimes doing it several times during this day with at least one of their stocks. Fortunes can be made with this kind of trading, but they can also be quickly lost. In order to get the day trading to work, you need to have a lot of experience and knowledge in your marketplace, a good strategy, and sufficient capital. You are not able to get into it at the last minute and you must be able to think clearly to keep your losses in check.

There are a number of benefits of going with day trading including:

- The potential profits that you can earn will be huge if you get more than one trade that is profitable during the day.

- The risk that comes with the stock or company changing are going to be reduced because you are not holding onto the stocks for that long. It is not likely that the company is going to change in just a day.

There are also a few cons that come with the day trading option, which is one of the reasons that people choose to go with one of the other methods of trading. Some of the cons that you will find with day trading include:

- You need to have an account balance that is pretty large before you can even get started.

- For those who are not used to working in the stock market and who can't control their emotions well can quickly lose a lot of money.

- Since you need to use a margin account, this type of trading can make you lose more money than you put in, which can be really dangerous in this option.

Momentum Trading

The next strategy that you may want to go with is

momentum trading. This is a strategy that the investor would use if the stocks are moving quickly, as well as on a high volume, going in one direction. When it comes to penny stocks, many of the investors are going to play on an upward momentum because these are not usually going to be available for a short sale.

Stocks that have momentum, it is because there is some buzz that is going on around the stock, such as through the news or because of rumors. To find these stocks, you will need to do some research and read through forums, message boards, and the news to find out what is going on. You should be able to find a few stocks that are getting quite a bit of attention at a time, which means that traders are going to be playing the stock pretty hard in order to get the price to go one way, and then they will take their profit before it all goes downward again.

There needs to be some research that goes into using this option. You need to take the time to watch how the activity for trading on the stock is doing before you make the purchase. Ones that have potential to be done with momentum are ones that have a really high volume and stocks that are moving either much higher or in the opposite direction compared to the market. You will be able to watch out for these signs by looking at charts, and watching the Level 2 quotes and the price action.

So after you have a list of the stocks that you would like to use, it is time to make the purchase. You will want to purchase it as quickly as possible, at as low of a price as possible, before the momentum starts to go down again. Once you own the penny stock, you need to be ready to go, watching the changes in the market, looking at charts, and seeing if there are any new filings or news. If you see that there is anything negative about the stock, such as bad news, bad indicators, or a negative trend, you should try to do a quick sell to cut the lasses before moving on; this is not an industry where you wait it out to see if it gets better.

On the other hand, if the momentum keeps going up, you will still need to hold on to the stocks and wait until some of the bids start to pile up. If the momentum is going up when you receive these bids and they are high enough for you to consider, you may want to go with one of them. The momentum can quit going up at any time and could start to go lower so take a bid that you are comfortable with before the tides start to turn. There may be a chance of earning more if you hold onto them longer, but if you hold on to long, you are going to lose it all so it is better to get what you can out of them.

Some of the benefits that you will be able to see with momentum trading include:

- The penny stocks are often going to be the ones that move the most when momentum starts to move, which means that you are able to make a lot of money in a short amount of time.

- You will be able to find a lot of information through message boards and other forums in order to pick the stocks that are right for you.

While this is a great way to make some good money in a short amount of time, there are also some cons that you will need to watch out for. Some of the cons of using momentum trading include:

- Sometimes the penny stocks are going to be volatile so your opportunity to sell and make a profit can be too short to earn anything.

- Companies that have dilution agendas can sometimes stall out a momentum run.

- There are some people who will use this idea in order to get more people to want their stocks. They will fake the buzz and the news so you need to be careful with working with them.

Swing Trading

Another option that you are able to work with is the swing trading. This type of trading is good if you are working on a stock that has the potential to move around in a short time period. This is usually going to be for stocks that will move within the day, but can go for up to four days. This is a type that will use a technical analysis in order to look for a stock that may have a momentum for their price over the short term. With this one, you are not going to be that interested in the values o the stock, but rather the trends and patterns of their price.

In a perfect market, the stocks are going to trade below or above a baseline value, or a moving average. The penny stocks are going to use this as both the resistance and support levels. When you are experimenting around with the charts, you will be able to see a set of moving averages will be fit to the actions of the price, and this can help out with the decisions during trading. Someone who has been in the stock market for some time would know that they should buy near the bottom of the moving average, but then they would sell before it reaches the target moving average.

There are quite a few pros that can come with this option include:

- This is a good style to use for beginners who are trying to get into the market and still makes some profits.

- Home runs are not usually going to be done with swing trading, but if you catch the beginning of a new uptrend, there is the possibility of getting large profits.

- You can use the basics of this kind of trading in any market that you would like. Big board stocks, futures, XCM, and Forex also use swing trading.

While there are quite a few positives that come with using penny stocks, there are also a few things that you need to watch out for. Swing trading is not an option that everyone is going to be fond of. Some of the cons of choosing swing trading as your strategy include:

- It is hard to find that perfect market where a particular stock is going to end up trading between the resistance and the support levels. This can get even harder to predict when there is a strong downtrend or a strong uptrend that are at work.

- Penny stocks can make it hard to time your buys the right way, especially when dealing with dilution on the stock that you purchased.

Technical Trading

Technical trading is a good option to go for when you are looking at all the points of your trading strategy. This one is going to use a Technical Analysis in order to help you find he right stocks that you would like to trade as well as helping you to set up your entry and then exit points to reduce losses if they would occur. Someone who picks to go with this kind of trading is going to use charts in order to examine the whole history of the stock, take the time to observe indicators that are going on, and then they will be able to identify the trends and patterns that are going on with the price.

There are a few different indicator groups that you can use in order to work with technical trading. Some of these include:

- Strength indicators: these are the indicators that are going to compare your current price to that of its history. This helps to show how weak or strong the stock will be. The Relative Strength Indicator is the most common one to use with this. Often it is shown as the top of your charts and it will indicate any overbought as well as oversold price conditions. Many times this can be a tip for helping you to buy and sell at the right price for a stock.

- Moving averages: these are known as MA's, and they are indicators that are going to be generated by averaging out the price levels over so much time. These can help you to see how often the movements of the stock are either below or above their averages. These are known as crossovers and can sometimes indicate breakdowns and breakouts as well, something that is important to a trader who is trying to pick out what stock they would like to work with.

- Pattern analysis: this is the evaluation of your charts in order to identify price formations, such as shapes, that come up in the history. Sometimes you are able to see wedges, triangles, cups, handles, and more for the stock you want to work with. these formations can sometimes be used to see into the future and determine if there is going to be any downward or upward movement. They are often caused by market forces, but one showing up, whether it is natural or not, will affect the action of that stock.

- Range analysis: this is where you are going to use a few different things together, such as the price range and the closing and opening prices in order to figure out where your resistance and support levels. These can help you to figure out what the best purchase as well as sell points are and can tell you other information, such as the levels of a breakdown and breakout with the stock.

- Gap analysis: this one is going to be done when you are able to find gaps in the charts you are looking at. A gap is going to be a spot that is inside the chart which will be caused by a price at the opening that is higher than what it was at the close the previous time period. The idea behind here is that these gaps are usually going to be filled so you will be able to use his in order to figure out the buy prices since you know that the price will go back down to fill up this gap before it goes higher.

All of these options are going to need you to use an analysis in order to figure out when to enter the market, how long to hold on to the penny stock, and when to let them go in order to make the biggest profit possible while limiting your losses. There are many benefits of using this kind of strategy including:

- There are many people who are on the forums and the boards who will help you to learn how to use TA and will talk to you about how to identify these hot stocks.

- Inside of penny stocks, these technical moves can be pretty strong. This is because TA is all there really is to help you to judge a stock and the way that the price will move.

Of course, while there are many people who will use this option to help them make decisions with their trading, there are a few cons that you will need to worry about. Some of these cons include:

- Bashers and pumpers can make almost all charts look like they are negative or positive, in the hopes of luring investors without experience into doing the action that they want.

- Without paying attention to some of the fundamentals, such as the news, a trade that looks good in this analysis could quickly turn around in just a few minutes and you could lose out.

- Using a technical analysis can be hard. It is complex and hard for some people to understand how to use.

Scalping

One of the other strategies that you can use when working in penny stocks is known as scalping. This is when the investor is going to make several trades throughout the day in order to make some small profits on one of the stocks that really doesn't move during that day. The scalper is going to use the bid and ask spread to make this work. They will buy their shares at the big, or somewhere close to it, they can then turn around and make a small profit. This one is not going to make them a ton of money, but it is better than nothing if you plan it out right and the market isn't moving.

You are able to repeat this kind of profit a few times in order to increase your profits. While you may only make a few dollars on each trade, when you do hundreds of these, you can make a lot of money through the day. This is sometimes considered day trading but be aware that all day trading is not scalping. Sometimes this strategy will do well, but you need to be careful because most stocks are not going to stay constant and you may end up with one that goes down in value through the day.

There are a few benefits that come from using the scalping method in your trading strategy. Some of these benefits include:

- For the most part, your penny stocks are going to have a large spread, which helps to give you a good profit.

- Penny stocks are sometimes going to trade sideways right after they finish with a big move or when they are trying to break through the resistance level.

- When you purchase at the bid and then sell right away at the ask, you will still get the lowest price on your purchase and it reduces the risk when you sell as quickly as possible before things can change.

Of course, there are a few negatives that can come up from using the scalping process for your penny stocks. Some of the cons of going with this method includes:

- Penny stocks can be difficult to do this with because of their anemic volume.

- This process is going to make you work against your market makers, and this makes it difficult.

- Since penny stocks are high risk and this option is only going to give you a small amount of profit, it may not be the best. If you want to give it a try it isn't bad, but some people don't think the risk is worth the reward.

All of these strategies have been used when it comes to working in penny stocks and it is important to figure out which method you would like to use for your needs. You can pick any of them and see some success, but you do need to be careful. You are not going to see the good results that you want if you are skipping all over the place and not sticking with a good strategy. Those who are the most successful with penny stocks, as well as with some of the other investing options are the ones who will pick out one strategy and stick with it. Consider some of the strategies that we talked about in this chapter and choose the one that works the best with your needs and will help you to make the biggest profit in penny stocks.

Chapter 5:

Top Tips of Working with Penny Stocks

As a beginner, you may be a bit worried about getting started with penny stocks. These are going to take a different route compared to working with traditional stock market options and sometimes it is hard to find the information that you need about the company before making the investment that you want. With that being said, it is possible to be successful when using penny stocks, you just need to be careful with the decisions that you make in penny stocks and take your time to really see results. Some of the tips that you can follow when you get started with penny stocks to help you be successful include:

Ignore some of the success stories

When you first get started with penny stocks, you are going to get a lot of information and emails about the success stories of others who have done well with penny stocks. These are found in social media sites and in emails, but often these are unusual circumstances or the information is all made up.

Instead of focusing on this, you need to look at the stocks on their own and see if they are going to work for you. Just ignore all of the success stories since most of these are going to be in order to get you to make a certain purchase. Do your research and learn about the market to determine which ones are the right ones for you.

Read through the disclaimers

If you are receiving a newsletter about the penny stocks, you need to be careful about the tips that you are reading. There is nothing wrong with picking out some of the stocks from these options, but you should be aware that most of them are sales tips and to give exposure to companies that, for the most part, are really bad and could end up making you lose a lot of money.

Most of the newsletters that you are going to pick won't give you the full story. The people who are writing them will do so in order to pump out the stock and they are not going to tell you the right time to sell the stocks. They will work hard to get you to purchase their stocks, and then you never hear from them again. It is fine to read through some of these to get some information, but when the disclaimers state that these are written as a promotion for one company or another, you know that the tips are more of a sales pitch rather than as good advice.

Sell quickly

One of the allures that you will hear about with penny stocks is that you are able to get a huge return on investment, up to 30 percent, in just a short amount of time. If you want to make a return on investment like this with penny stocks, you will need to sell your stocks quickly after you purchase them. Unfortunately, instead of being happy with the 30 percent or so, people will get greedy and will look to make a huge return. Considering penny stocks are sometimes getting pumped out and the industry are volatile, you should be happy with what you get or you may lose out on a lot of money.

Be careful when listening to the company management

You need to be really careful about the people you are listening to inside of penny stocks, even when it comes to company management of the stock that you are working with. These companies are trying to work in order to get the stocks up. When the stocks up, these companies are able to raise more money and it is more likely they will stay in business. In some instances, they may not even be companies, but basically insiders who are trying to get rich.

In fact, most of the promotions that you will see come from the same group of people who will use different companies and press releases in order to get some hype up and make some extra money. They may have purchased the stocks at a lower price and now want to create a lot of buzz to get you to make a purchase much higher than what they paid.

In between the people who are using pump and dump to make money and the companies who are worried about going under and want to get you to agree with them to save them from failing, it is hard to know which penny stocks are safe. You need to think independent of the news and some of the promotions that you hear before picking out the stocks that you want to invest in. With some good research and being critical of things you hear, it is easier to pick out the penny stocks that are actually good and to make the money you want.

Focus on high volume

When you are getting started, it is best to only use stocks that have a minimum of 100,000 shares traded each day. If you go with a stock that is too low in volume, it is sometimes too hard to get yourself out of this issue. In addition, experts recommend that you pick out the stocks that are selling for over 50 cents a share. Going with a stocks that are lower in price than this may seem appealing, but often these aren't considered liquid enough to really play with. But if you pick out stocks that are getting more than 100,000 shares a day traded and they are over 50 cents for each share, you are going to have more luck getting them to sell nicely.

Pick the best stock out of the bunch

You should make sure that you pick out one of the best stocks that you can find, especially when you are a beginner in this industry. Some experts recommend that you find a stock that have really good earnings overall or one that has broken out of its average 52 week highs in volume. Some of these are easy to find, but the trick with these is that you want to find ones that have these highs, but not because of a pump and dump scheme. You want the highs to be because others are interested in the stock and the value is going up naturally, not because of some buzz that is created to inflate the price.

Never fall in love with just one stock

When it comes to the stock market and with penny stocks, you can't fall in love with one stock. When you decide that one stock, and only one, is the option that you will go with, you are going to end up failing. You won't look at the stock in an objective way and this can make it hard to stick with your guns and make sure that you are thinking about profit.

There are always going to be salespeople who can come to you with a great story about their company and will make you fall in love with their product. But your job is to look at something objectively to find out if it is actually going to make you the money that is promises. With some good research and hard work, you will be able to find the right options for your needs without falling prey to others who want your money.

Do your research

Before you get into any of the stocks, you need to make sure that you complete your research. There is not much information that is provided inside of the penny stocks, although there are a few companies that will provide this information to help you out. This means that you will need to get to work and do some research. Look up the company and learn a bit about them including some press releases and other news that surrounds them. You should take a look at the market overall and see where things are going. You can even look at the current stock and see its history to learn how things are going for the company.

When you finish the right research before making a decision, you will find that it is easier than ever to get the results that you want. You will be able to make informed decisions, rather than just jumping into the mix and hoping that it all works out for the best.

Keep your head

If you are new to penny stocks, you may find that it is easy to get really involved with the stocks. You may get too involved, feeling that you need to keep going when you are loosing money and getting too upset, or too happy, when things aren't going the way that you want. It is important to look at all of this objectively and learn how to always keep your head and think critically, no matter what is going on in the market.

For those who loose their tempers quickly, those who have an addictive personality, or those who will have trouble with these almost gambling like options, it is not a good idea to get into penny stocks. You need to be able to take control of the situation, no matter what happens, so that you can think critically and make decisions that will help you to make the most money possible with penny stocks.

When you are first getting started with penny stocks, you may be worried about how you will get to the top and start earning money with this kind of market. Follow some of these simple steps so that you can learn how to work with penny stocks and get them to work for you.

Chapter 6:

SEC Regulations on Penny Stocks

Since the penny stocks are not traded on the stock market, they are going to have some different rules compared to those companies. With that being said, the SEC has stepped in a bit to add some rules to the penny stocks in order to protect the company as well as to protect the investor a little bit. Here we are going to take a look at some of the SEC regulations for this investment type.

The first one is that the broker or the dealer must approve the transaction of all their investors first with an agreement that is written out from the investor as the basis of approval. The SEC is going to require this practice to help prevent manipulative and fraudulent practices. What this means is that the broker is going to check to see if the investor is suitable for trading in penny stocks by looking at their objectives, their experience in investing, and even their financial position.

Next, the investor is going to receive a disclosure that will detail the risks that come with investing in penny stocks. This disclosure most including the fraud remedies, the broker duties, the concepts that are used in penny stocks, and the investor rights in this process.

Then the broker must provide another disclosure to the investor about the bid and offer quotes at some time before the investor does any trading in penny stocks. The point of this discloser is that it helps the investor to monitor the price movement of their stocks. If the broker does not provide this disclosure to the investor, it is illegal.

The broker or the dealer also needs to let the investor know how much they are going to earn from each of the transactions that the investor is going to be earning. This helps you as the investor to determine if the transaction is actually one that is in your best interest or if it is the one that gives the broker the highest payout when you are done.

The broker is also responsible for providing statements each month about the account status of the investor. These statements must include the number and the identity of all the penny stocks that are owned by that investor. It should include the purchase price, the market value (or at least an estimate), and the transaction date of the security to help the investor keep track of what is going on.

The idea behind all of these is that the SEC wants to make sure that the investor is not being tricked into making purchases in penny stocks without being fully informed about what is going on with them.

Conclusion

Thank for making it through to the end of *Penny Stocks: A Complete Guide to Buy And Trade Penny Stocks*. Let's hope it was informative and able to provide you with all of the tools you need to achieve your goals of

The next step is to find a broker you would like to use and get started with penny stocks. It is always a good idea to have a plan in place to help you to get started before just jumping in. Penny stocks are a bit harder compared to working with your traditional stock market, but it is a great way to make some money and see your portfolio grow.

Inside this guidebook, we took some time to discuss the penny stocks and how you would get started with them. We discussed how penny stocks are different than the traditional stock market before moving on to some of the tips that you can follow in order to get into the market for penny stocks. Then we spent a good deal of time talking about the different strategies that you can use when getting into penny stocks. The strategy is one of the most important steps to getting this started because it helps you to know what to look for when making your predictions and making money. We will then end with some great tips, as well as an overview of the SEC regulations on the penny stocks to help you fully understand what is going on with this industry.

When you are ready to get into investing or you are looking for a new way to expand out the portfolio and make some more money, penny stocks may be the answer that you are looking for. Make sure to look through this guidebook and learn as much as possible about working in penny stocks and how you can make money in this market.

Finally, if you found this book useful in any way, a review on Amazon is always appreciated!

Penny Stocks

How To Start Trading Penny Stocks

Alvin Williams

Introduction

Congratulations on downloading this book and thank you for doing so.

The following chapters will discuss everything you need to know about penny stocks, and how you can become a successful trader. You will learn what penny stocks are, how to identify the best penny stocks to invest in, as well as the common pitfalls that you should be aware of, and more!

There are plenty of books on this subject on the market, thanks again for choosing this one! Every effort was made to ensure it is full of as much useful information as possible, please enjoy!

Chapter 1:

Understanding Penny Stocks

As discussed in the first book, penny stocks are stocks that have a value of less than $5 per share. In the United Kingdom, any stock that costs less than £1 is considered a penny stock. Penny stocks are also referred to as cent stocks or penny shares.

Because penny stocks have a relatively low value, they are mostly traded by small and start-up companies. However, you can still find a few big and well-established companies that trade penny stocks on major market exchanges.

Trading penny stocks vs. gambling

Some people think that trading penny stocks is similar to gambling, for good reasons: First, the high volatility of penny stocks can be likened to a game of slots in a casino where you can quickly lose your money or earn a big amount within a short period of time. Second, with so many factors that affect the prices of penny stocks, these stocks have a highly speculative value — just like casino games, which are very speculative. Last but not least, majority of people who invest in penny stocks lose their money, which is the normal state of things in the casino.

However...

Unlike casino games, the outcome of every trade does not come from a shuffled deck of cards or a mere random generator. Every result is caused by the market movement, which comes from real people and businesses. Therefore, unlike a game of slots where you depend on pure luck to earn money, trading penny slots lets you examine economic indicators and other factors that greatly influence the outcome of any trade. This means that if you know the proper way to approach every trade that you make, if you know the right strategies to use and have the correct data to analyze, you can significantly increase your chances of success by more than 80%.

Of course, if you do not exert any serious effort or research and simply trade penny stocks by merely relying on pure luck, then you are gambling. But, if you want to be a professional trader and make a living trading penny stocks - if you are willing to spend hours of research and study to analyze the market movement and identify the best stocks - then that is not gambling but investing.

Is trading penny stocks for you?

Penny stocks have a high volatility. Their prices can fluctuate dramatically within a short period of time, and such changes in their prices are considered normal. On the one hand, the high volatility of penny stocks can cause a penny stock that has a value of $3 today to have a value of less than a dollar in the next few days. On the other hand, such high volatility of penny stocks can make them double, triple, or even increase their value to more than 15 times in just a short period of time.

As the saying goes: "The higher the risk, the higher the return." In the same manner, the lower the risk, the lower is the return. Trading penny stocks is considered a high-risk investment, counterbalanced by its high-profit potential. If you do not want a high-risk investment, you might do well with blue-chip stocks. However, the return will also be lower. But, if you do not mind the risk, if you want to grow your investment to more than thrice its value within a short period of time, then trading penny stocks could be the best decision you can ever make.

If you have more than enough funds available, you can get the best of both worlds by investing a part of your funds in penny stocks and applying the rest to buy some blue-chip stocks.

Penny stocks vs. blue-chip stocks

Penny stocks and blue-chip stocks are issued by companies. Although both are considered stocks, there are significant differences between the two.

Volatility

Unlike penny stocks, blue-chip stocks have low volatility. This means that their prices do not usually fluctuate as much, which makes them very stable. However, such low volatility also means having a low-profit potential.

Sensitivity

Sector influences easily affect the prices of penny stocks, which is one of the reasons why penny shares are very volatile. Blue-chip stocks are more stable and are not easily affected by sector influences.

Profit potential

On the one hand, to earn a lot with blue-chip stocks, you will have to invest more money. Although investing in blue-chip stocks is more secure, the profit potential is also low. A 50% increase is already considered high. On the other hand, investing in penny stocks has a much higher profit potential. An increase of 50% is considered normal. In fact, if you get really lucky, the value of your penny stocks can increase by more than 20 times.

Speculative

Blue-chip stocks have little to no speculative value, while the value of penny stocks is very speculative. There are so many factors that affect the prices of penny stocks, and many of which are outside your control.

Dividends

If you are a holder of blue-chip stocks, then you can expect to receive dividends from the company.

However, if you are a holder of penny stocks, you would barely receive any dividends.

Availability of data

The information that you can get when you research about penny stocks is limited. Penny stocks are not as transparent as blue-chip stocks. This makes their value harder to speculate. Blue-chip stocks are more open and transparent. Many companies reveal their books and financial data, which can help you gauge if the company is doing well or not.

Penny stock volatility

If there is one thing that penny stocks are known for, it is their high volatility. If you take a look at the penny stock market, you will notice that huge price swings are normal, and they happen within a short period of time.

But, what does *volatility* mean? Volatility means quick and unpredictable changes. Hence, when we say that penny stocks have high volatility, it means that their prices change dramatically and rapidly.

The high volatility of penny stocks cuts both ways:

- Their high volatile nature makes their prices difficult to predict; therefore, you can easily lose money by investing in the wrong penny shares.

- Their high volatility is what causes the big price swings; therefore, there is a good opportunity to earn a big profit.

Before you start trading, it is important for you to know the causes behind the high volatility of penny stocks by looking at the factors that strongly affect their prices:

Traders themselves

Every time a trader buys or sells a penny stock, it has an impact on the price movement of the stock concerned. Traders, of course, have their own preferences as to when to buy or sell their stocks, including which penny stocks they will buy or sell; and this is something that you cannot control.

Volatile nature

When you deal with penny stocks, you need to realize that you do not just deal with stocks or graphs that you see on the computer. Instead, you deal with real people and businesses. The market is volatile in nature because it is alive. Therefore, you can expect continuous changes to take place.

Consumer behavior

For any business to succeed, it all depends on consumer behavior. The consumers are the main customers of a business (except, of course, in the case of a B-to-B enterprise). But every consumer has his own preferences and prejudices, and they also change. A product that is happily accepted by the market today may be completely forgotten tomorrow.

Government laws and policies

Governments have an active interest in businesses. In fact, they even enact laws to encourage investors to make an investment. Of course, they also gain benefits from businesses, such as being able to provide employment to their citizens, as well as the money that they receive from taxes. Government laws and policies affect the volatility of penny stocks because their laws can directly affect businesses. They exercise a strong influence over businesses and investors, and can even direct market behavior.

Economic problems

When the economy is not doing well, businesses also fail to make a good profit. This usually results in a significant decrease in the prices of penny stocks. This is one of the reasons why economic problems should be resolved at the first instance. Economic problems will not just pull down the values of various penny stocks, but can also adversely affect the lives of the people.

Reports

Financial reports of publicly-traded companies are released periodically. These reports are open to the public, and traders use them to find out the best penny stocks to invest in. However, it is worth noting that although these reports are good factors to be considered, they are not sufficient to guarantee the success of a trade. Still, when these reports are released, they tend to influence the decisions of many investors, which affect the volatility of stocks.

Competition

Competition is good for consumers because it compels businesses to only offer the best quality of products and services. Competition can also be beneficial to businesses by compelling them to improve and grow. However, as one business wins against its competitors and increases the value of its stocks, this diminishes the value of the stocks of its competitors. This, of course, will affect the prices of penny stocks in the market.

These factors, among others, greatly influence the prices of penny stocks, which explains the high volatility of the penny stock market. This makes the prices of penny stocks difficult to predict with certainty. Not only are there many factors to consider, but even a single element has a potential to create a significant change in the prices of penny stocks.

Take advantage of price swings

Although the high volatility of penny stocks is what discourages some investors, it is also this same reason that makes it an attractive investment. It is the dramatic price swings that will enable you to double, triple, or even multiply your investment by more than 20 times.

Although you can trade penny stocks within a single day, it is not uncommon to see traders who wait for days or weeks before they sell their stocks. Since high volatility is a major characteristic of penny stocks, you can expect their value to rise. Unfortunately, there is also a probability that their value may drop significantly.

Chapter 2:

Risks and Benefits

There are two things that trading penny stocks are very much known for:

- You can quickly make a big amount of money.

- There is a high probability that you will lose your investment.

These are two opposing extremes that you will be facing. Of course, your objective is to rake in serious profits. Unfortunately, the majority of people who trade penny stocks fail to make any positive return. In fact, they lose their money. But do not be discouraged; because there are still people out there, the well-experienced and real expert traders who double, triple, and continuously grow their money more than you can ever imagine.

Losing a trade is normal. Even well-experienced traders make the wrong investment decisions from time to time. However, you must avoid such mistakes as much as possible. Now, in order to help cut down your future losses, you should be aware of the risks that you will be facing when you trade penny stocks.

The risks

Small companies

The majority of the companies in the penny stock market are small companies. In fact, they can be so small that they do not even meet the minimum capitalization requirement. You will find many of these companies on the Pink Sheets. But then again, as discussed in the previous book, do not buy penny stocks from the Pink Sheets. Since they are small companies, it is hard to tell if they are stable enough and if they will even grow. Many small companies also tend to be less professional. Sometimes the executives of a small company see and treat the assets of the company, including the stocks and penny shares, as their own personal belonging.

Start-up companies

Many of the companies that issue penny stocks are the start-up companies. Therefore, they tend to have a very limited history that you can track. This makes it risky because you would not know for sure if the business is legitimate or if the company is operating a scam.

Less transparent

Penny stocks do not have stringent requirements. You can always buy them on the Pink Sheets or over the counter (OTC). Remember that the companies on the Pink Sheets are not required to file with the SEC and to meet the minimum capitalization requirements or capital stock of a legitimate company.

Many companies on the Pink Sheets only reveal very limited information about their business, so it is hard to get sufficient and accurate data. Worse, some companies operate a scam.

Bankruptcy

The penny stock market is not only participated by small and start-up companies, it also has companies that are about to go bankrupt. Unfortunately, these struggling companies will not reveal that they are already about to declare bankruptcy and will even make their stocks to look like an attractive investment. Of course, there is still a probability to make a good amount of profit when you invest in a company that is struggling to survive, especially when the company is able to save itself from bankruptcy and begin to grow successfully. However, the probability for such ideal scenario to happen is small. Trading penny stocks is already risky enough; you would not want to take more risks.

The reason why you should not invest in a company that is about to go bankrupt is because you will run the risk of losing everything. Once the company declares bankruptcy and does not have sufficient assets to cover all its debts and obligations to its creditors, you will not be able to get your money back.

Low liquidity

Penny stocks have low liquidity. With a low liquidity, they become open to manipulation. A common type of fraudulent scheme is the pump and dump, in which the value of certain penny stocks are pumped up using some fraudulent marketing hype in order to convince traders to buy them. As its name already implies, the price of certain stocks are pumped up using some promotional or marketing hype. In turn, traders will find the stocks attractive and make an investment. The penny stocks are then dumped on the traders and their value begins to fall down.

Take note that the pump and dump scheme can be applied even if the company is actually doing well. In fact, when the company is making profits, the pump and dump scheme will be harder to detect. By adding a few dollars on the price of certain stocks that are already increasing, it is almost impossible for traders to determine whether the increased total value is due to legitimate means or merely a result of a pump and dump scheme.

Speculative

Due to so many factors that affect the prices of penny stocks, it can be said that the penny stock market is highly speculative. An important thing in trading penny stocks is to first buy the stocks that truly have a good value. Unfortunately, with the increasing number of scams, hackers, and frauds out there, it becomes difficult to know whether you are really purchasing a good stock or merely a stock whose value is being pumped. Second, even if you get to buy a profitable stock, there are many active factors that can affect its performance in the market. The best stock today may no longer be considered a good stock by tomorrow, depending on the circumstances. Also, granting that the prices of your penny stocks increase, will the buyers still see them attractive and profitable by the time you want to sell them?

These, among many other things, are the risks faced by traders of penny stocks. Consider also the sad fact that most traders fail to make any profit and simply lose their investment.

Do you think you are up for the challenge? If your entrepreneurial spirit is not crushed by these risks, then get ready for the awesome benefits of trading penny stocks.

The Benefits

Trading penny stocks is one of the best investment opportunities that offer wonderful benefits. So, if you honestly think that you can manage the above mentioned risks, then welcome to the world of high profits — a place where you can double, triple, or even multiply your money by more than 20 times in a short period of time.

Price

Penny stocks are cheap. A single penny stock only costs less than $5. If you have a lot of money to invest, then you can have thousands of stocks of different companies. If you are on a shoestring budget, then this opportunity is also available to you.

High potential return

When you trade penny stocks, there is a potential to multiply the value of your stocks many times over. In fact, there is a potential for the prices of your stocks to double within 24 hours or less.

Unlike blue-chip stocks where a 60% increase is considered a big profit already, such is considered normal when you trade penny stocks. And, unlike binary options where you can gain 90% but has a much higher risk, trading penny stocks can make your money grow by more than 500% within a short period of time. Also, since the penny stock market is mostly composed of small businesses, there is a high probability for the value of their penny stocks to grow, since small businesses have a lot of space for improvements.

High volume

You can have thousands of penny stocks for a small amount. Having a high volume of penny stocks is good, especially if you get them from a start-up company that is doing well.

Low or controlled risk

Penny stocks are inexpensive. You do not have to purchase a lot of penny stocks to earn a decent amount of profit. You can also diversify your stocks to help minimize your losses. And, unlike trading binary options where you will lose your whole wager when you make a wrong investment decision, you can still keep your penny stocks and sell them. If you are patient enough, there is really no such thing as a permanent loss. Considering the volatility of penny stocks, even if the value of your penny stocks decreases, there is a good chance that it will increase after some time.

Chapter 3:

Best Trading Practices

No matter what strategy you use, there are best practices that all experienced and successful traders observe. These are the keys that will help you succeed. These things are not just something that you read because their true essence is in doing, so be sure to apply them to your every trade. Here are the best trading practices that you should know:

Do your research

Do not simply focus on the penny stocks that you want to purchase. Keep in mind that the performance of stocks heavily depends upon the overall performance of the business. Therefore, you must also give attention to the company itself. How is the company doing in the market? Does it match up well against its competitors? Remember to research the penny stocks that you intend to purchase, as well as the company concerned.

The scope of research is, if course, a big task. This is

one of the most important parts of trading. Also find out the factors that affect a particular stock and understand them. Are these factors present at the current moment? Is there any chance that any of these influential factors appear in the future? If so, what are the consequences? The more research and knowledge that you have the better is your chances of investing in the right penny stocks.

Only invest the money you can afford to lose

A very common advice known to all gamblers is this: "Only play with the money you can afford to lose." This is a common advice given to gamblers. Although trading penny stocks may not be considered gambling, especially if you do not rely on pure luck, it is still similar to gambling in the sense that there is always the possibility to lose your money. Do not use the money that you need for your child's enrollment or for paying the household bills, etc. Although there is no assurance that you will lose you money, you must only invest the money that you can afford to lose. The penny stock market is very volatile that it is hard to guarantee that you will make a profit.

Set a limit

It is a sound advice, especially for beginners, to decide before making any trade on a limit on how long will you continue to hold on to a losing stock, as well as for a profitable one. The penny stock market is extremely volatile. Although you can expect for their value to increase and decrease almost randomly, it does not always mean that a stock whose price has just decreased will soon increase.

Part of the volatility of penny stocks is that a significant decrease in value can still be followed by another big drop. Therefore, in order to cut down your losses, it is important to set a limit on how long would you be willing to hold on to a losing stock. In the same way, you should know how long you will hold on to a winning stock. Again, even if a stock continuously experiences an increase in value, there is still the possibility that its price can just drop dramatically, almost without any warning.

Look for patterns

The movement of the prices of penny stocks can be

said to be like random. The thing is, randomness creates patterns. And, if it is not random, then there is more possibility to find a pattern. If you can identify these patterns early, then you will be one step ahead. Just remember, though, that patterns are like trends; and in the world of penny stocks, they do not last for very long.

Observe the trends

Analyze the graphs and tables that show the performance of certain penny stocks. Do not just study their current record, but also check their past performance. This is a good way for you to know if the stocks are really doing well or not. Also, do not rely completely on the latest trends. Although the latest trends can show you the most recent performances of penny stocks, you must take note that trends often change. In fact, in the penny stock market, you will barely see a trend that will last for too long.

Know the latest news

If you are serious about trading penny stocks, then you should be updated on the latest news. The many factors that affect the prices of penny stocks are usually revealed on the news. Although the news would not state it directly, you should know that laws, businesses, economy, market behavior, and inflation, among others, can affect the prices of penny stocks. Take note, however, that although the news can give you valuable insights and information, what matters the most is still the actual prices of penny stocks.

Stay calm

Bad days do happen, and you may encounter a series of losing streaks despite doing some good research. During such moment, or the moment when you first experience your first loss, stay calm. I repeat: stay calm. The penny stock market does not care about how you feel, so must remain objective and focused. If you cannot control yourself, just quickly turn off your computer or mobile phone.

Do not be greedy

Especially for beginners, it is recommended that you stick to getting small yet regular profits. Many inexperienced traders lose their money not because of buying the wrong penny stocks, but because of keeping the stocks for too long. Do not underestimate the high volatile nature of the penny stock market. Learn to sell, cash out, and enjoy your profit.

Keep your emotion under control

Do not be an emotional trader. Although it is good to feel passionate about trading penny stocks, do not let your passion blind your judgment. Never make any trade when under pressure and treat trading penny stocks as a business.

Make your own decision

Although it is advisable to read the opinions of "experts," it is wrong to let them dictate your investment decisions. Unfortunately, many of these so-called "experts" are hacks and frauds. They promote themselves as an expert even if their overall losses outweigh their profits. Of course, there are still a few real experts out there, but even the best traders still commit mistakes from time to time. After all, the process of developing your trading strategy is a life-long journey.

Instead of relying on expert advice, you should develop your own understanding of the penny stock market and make your own decisions. You can compare your decisions with the pieces of advice given by "experts" and see how well you match up. Of course, you also need to check the real outcome of a particular trade to see if you have made the right investment decision.

Do not chase after your losses

This is another advice given to gamblers. Unfortunately, although this advice is very common, many still fail to observe it. There are several ways to chase after your losses, but they all usually lead to the same unfortunate result. Usually, you chase after your losses by investing more right after you lose a trade. When you lose, you simply have this strong urge to get your money back. Another thing people do is by continuously holding on to losing stocks, thinking that once they sell them, they would no longer save their lost investment. In any way, you are on the losing side with just a little hope of getting your losses back. The bad thing here is that you gamble your whole funds for the sake of recovering a few losses. Therefore, the risk is really high.

A good way to avoid this is by learning to accept your losses. If certain penny stocks fail to meet your expectations, learn to accept your losses by selling them and starting over again. When you seriously engage in trading penny stocks, losing some investments is normal. After all, once you get lucky and hit truly profitable stocks, you will quickly recover all your losses and enjoy grand profits.

Stick to your strategy

During the execution process, you must do your best to stick to your planned strategy; otherwise, you will not be able to measure effectiveness, as well as its full potential. Of course, there are instances that you should abandon your strategy, especially if circumstances clearly show that continuing with your strategy will result in a total loss of investment.

Only invest in penny stocks that have a high volume

According to some "expert," you should only invest in stocks that trade at least a hundred thousand shares per day. This serves as a safeguard against the risk of being illiquid.

Pump your stocks

There is a reason why the pump and dump scheme still exists despite many people being aware of such scheme: It works.

So, if you do not mind being a bit tricky, you can market yourself as an "expert" in trading penny stocks. You can put up a website and send out newsletters to your readers. You can then purchase cheap penny stocks, use your connections to gain interest in the stocks, and sell them at a premium price. If you are the type that can convince people to do what you want, then this may be an easy way for you to make money. However, if you are the type who cannot exercise a bit of trickery (which is a very good thing about you), then you can simply take advantage of people who pump and dump their stocks. How? Simply buy their penny stocks, preferably before they pump them or as early as possible while they pump their value. You can then wait for their price to increase, sell your penny stocks, and reap some profits.

Keep a journal

Writing a journal is not required, but it is very helpful. You do not have to be a professional writer to write a journal. What is important is for you to be honest about everything that you write.

There are many things that you can write in your journal. It is also good to write your goals and reasons for why you want to trade penny stocks. Also, write any lessons and mistakes that you have learned. It is your journal, so feel free to write about anything and everything about your trading adventure. A journal will allow you to think outside the box and be a smarter trader.

Take a break

Trading penny stocks has a gambling factor: It can be addicting. It is something that you can do for hours without being tired. You would feel more like playing than working. However, when you engage in research, which is a must, that is the time where you will definitely feel that trading penny stocks involve serious work. Allow yourself to take a break from to time. Remember that you will have a better mental clarity if you give yourself a chance to take a rest.

Get the latest updates quickly

Successful traders get the latest news and respond quickly. The way to take advantage of the impact of the news on the prices of stocks is by making the appropriate trading actions just before others realize them. For example, when you see that your penny stocks will soon encounter a massive drop in value, sell them right away. Also, if possible, know the news before it is even released in the public. To increase the probability that certain stocks will increase in value, the stocks should also be effectively promoted. Therefore, it is helpful if you can join and be active on online groups and forums on penny stocks.

Focus on start-up companies

One of the best things about the penny stock market is that it is a place where you can find many start-up companies. Surely, a good number of these companies will do well. Unfortunately, some of them will perform badly and even get bankrupt. However, if you manage to get the stocks of the good start-up companies early on, you will find yourself in a winning position.

Therefore, you must exert the effort to research and analyze the different start-up companies that participate in the penny stock market. When analyzing a particular company, also measure how it matches up against its competitors in the market.

Growing companies have lots of space for improvements; and as their profits increase and they continue to expand, the prices of their penny stocks also increase.

Have fun

It is a common advice that you should choose a job that you enjoy. In the same way, you should enjoy trading penny stocks. If you do not enjoy it, then maybe it is a signal that you should just invest somewhere else. Also, you can make better decisions when you are having fun.

Choose the right penny stocks

Always choose the right penny stocks to invest in. How do you know the right ones? Sufficient research. Never commence a trade without sufficient research. Take note that a little research is not enough. Researches made without serious efforts are only as good as a mere toss of a coin. Also, the most profitable and attractive-looking stocks may not always be the right penny stocks to invest in. After all, no matter what the media says, the numbers on the penny stock market are what counts.

Be patient

Patience is important when you trade penny stocks. Do not hurry to make a buy order simply because you have funds in your account. Also, many times, to take advantage of the high volatility of penny stocks, you will have to wait for some time. Take note that every action that you make is essential. The stocks that you buy today are the stocks that you will soon sell. Be patient, wait for the proper timing, and act accordingly.

Use the high volatility to your advantage

Although many people shy away from penny stocks due to their high volatility, it is this volatile nature of penny stocks that make them a profitable investment. With high volatility, mastering the famous principle for making money is the key to profit: buy when the price is low, and sell when the price is high.

Chapter 4:

Start Trading

The only way to truly understand how to trade penny stocks is by actual application. If you think that you are ready to face the challenges and enjoy the immense benefits of trading penny stocks, then it is time for you to get in the game and make your first trade.

What to look for in a penny stock broker

In order to trade penny stocks, you will need a broker. It is easy to find brokers online. In fact, simply by doing a quick search online you will find so many penny stock brokers. But, with so many penny stock brokers out there, how can tell which ones can give you the best quality of service? Here are the criteria to look for:

Transaction fee

This refers to the cost of trading, which is usually imposed per trade that you make. The amount of transaction charges can be a bit tricky. Some brokers offer a lower transaction fee only as a promo to get you sign up on the site, but then impose a more expensive rate after the promo period.

Surcharge

This is a small amount usually imposed on every share that is under a dollar, while some impose it for shares under $3, depending on the broker. Although surcharges are usually very little, you should be mindful of them because they pile up quickly. For example, if you have 100,000 shares with a $0.01 surcharge for every share, you will have a total surcharge of $1,000. Also, when you trade penny stocks, you will usually have to buy lots of stocks in order to get significant profits.

Trading restrictions

You should be able to trade and manage your account on your own. This means that the platform should not require you to call or send a message just to make a trade. You should be able to trade on your own with a few clicks of a mouse, without having to ask for any permission from the broker. Do not worry; this should not be a problem, especially when you choose to work trustworthy and well-established brokers.

Volume restrictions

Do not choose a broker that imposes a restriction as to how many shares you can trade or would impose a high charge for a trading a high volume of penny stocks. After all, you will have a high surcharge fee when you trade in a high volume.

Trading frequency rate

As already mentioned, there are brokers that impose a small transaction fee per trade. Although there is nothing wrong with it, some brokers will impose a higher rate of transaction fee if you fail to trade a certain number of times within a given period, to be specified by the broker. Although this would not be a problem if you trade on a regular basis, this can be an issue if you only trade sporadically.

Minimum deposit requirements

The required minimum deposit before you can start actual trading varies from broker to broker. Most platforms will require you to deposit around $100-

$250 before you can trade. If you just want to test the water and think that the amount is too high, you might want to try depositing using bitcoins. A bitcoin is a cryptocurrency, and most sites that accept bitcoins also accept a very low minimum deposit provided that you use bitcoins.

Mobile trading

Ideally, you should be able to manage your account and make a trade simply by using your mobile phone. This will allow you to trade anytime and anywhere without having to use a computer.

Rating and reviews

Before you sign up for an account with any trading platform or broker, you should first examine the broker's rating, as well as the reviews left by other traders. Take note of the dates of the latest reviews. If the last reviews are dated about a year ago, then be cautious even if the last reviews are positive reviews. To increase your chances of having a good experience, only deal with legitimate brokers.

Banking

You need to take note of a broker's banking features. You must be able to deposit and withdraw your money easily and quickly. Also, many brokers offer more deposit options, but only have limited options for making a withdrawal. This part is very important to take note of; otherwise, you run the risk of not being able to withdraw your money.

Withdrawal fee

This is a small amount imposed by your broker each time you make a withdrawal.

Create an account

In order to trade penny stocks, you need to sign up for an investment trading account with a penny stock broker. Registration is fast and easy. Not all brokers are the same, so make a comparison of the brokers and choose the one that will best suit your needs.

Here is a list of famous platforms that you check. Take note that this list is not exclusive and there is no guarantee as to their quality of service. This is because the management team and strategy can change from time to time. A good broker today may be the worst broker tomorrow. Also, keep your eye on new and upcoming brokers.

Charles Schwab (www.schwab.com)

E*Trade (us.etrade.com)

TradeKing (www.tradeking.com)

Interactive Brokers (www.interactivebrokers.com.hk)

Scottrade (www.scottrade.com)

TD Ameritrade (www.tdameritrade.com)

OptionsHouse (www.optionshouse.com)

Demo play

Most platforms offer free virtual credits for a demo play. Although this will not make you earn any real money, a demo play is good to have a taste of what trading is like before you use any real cash. A demo play can also be used to test your strategy. Hence, it is a good way to help cut down your losses.

Start small

Whether you have funded your account with a huge amount of money or not, starting out small is strongly recommended, especially for beginners. Many traders rush and wager a big amount, so they can earn high amounts of profit. Unfortunately, to increase your chances of success in trading penny stocks, you need to exert serious efforts, research, and even experience. Actual trading is different from what you read in books. Books can merely describe what trading is like, but actual trading is more challenging.

Increase your success rate

Regardless which strategy in the first book that you intend to use, you can increase your rate of success by observing the following pieces of advice. The proper way to apply the following is by actual application.

Fundamental analysis

This is the same strategy used in binary options. Take note that the graphs that you see on your computer are not the actual penny stock market. They are, in fact, the result of what takes place in the actual market. When you do fundamental analysis, you need to analyze the businesses themselves, the economy, the news, and other things that can have an impact on the prices of penny stocks. It is important to focus on the companies because the success of the companies also reflects the price movements of their penny stocks. If a company is doing well, the prices of its penny stocks will also tend to increase.

Limit your orders

Set a limit order so you will not have to keep watch on your computer every minute just to monitor the prices of penny stocks. This also applies both when you make a buy order as well as a sell order. In case of a buy order, limiting your order will help you avoid overpayment. In case of a sell order, this will make you sell your stocks automatically provided your selling price is accepted. Of course, if your set price is not reached, you still keep your stocks and try again.

Stop-loss limit

A stop-loss limit is an effective to prevent you from chasing your losses. Take note that the proper way to apply a stop-loss limit is by setting it before you even commence a trade, regardless whether it is a buy or a sell order. Also, remember that the penny stock market is highly volatile that having a stop-loss limit can be considered a must. So, how does it work? Say, for example, you set a limit of 35%, if the value of your stock drops and reaches 35%, you should accept your losses and make a sell order. Although it is not uncommon to see the prices of penny stocks increasing and decreasing, it is also usual for their prices to experience a dramatic and continuous increase in price. And, many times, continuously clinging to a losing stock, especially if the circumstances show a glaring loss, is the worst decision you can make.

Keep your profit

It is important that you cash out. Yes, sell and cash out. Remember that the only way that the profits on the screen can really mean something is only when you turn them into real cash. As long as they are only on the screen, they are just numbers and are only like the credits that you use when you do a demo play.

Of course, you do not have to cash out everything. A good way is to set a certain percentage, for example, 10% of every successful trade. This means that you will cash out every 10% of each successful trade that you make. This is also a good way to cut down your losses.

Focus on the numbers

No matter what everybody says, the only thing that matters is the numbers that appear on the penny stock market. So, focus on the numbers. Even if a particular stock is being heavily promoted, if you do not see any change in value, you should not consider it a good investment. Also, words can easily be twisted, especially during a marketing hype. Numbers are harder to manipulate.

Reassess your strategy

There is one thing that strongly characterizes the penny stock market: change. Therefore, you need to reassess your strategy from time to time; and see to it that your strategy matches up with the market changes. The high volatility of penny stocks cannot be underestimated, and the changes that it makes have a strong impact on your investment.

Lighten your position

If the value of certain penny stocks experiences a good increase but you notice that the stocks are no longer being promoted or that the news about them has stopped, you should lighten your position by selling your stocks before their value decreases. If there are reasons to believe that their price will continuously increase, then you can just cash out a percentage of those stocks, for example, 50%.

Learn from your mistakes

Mistakes are a normal part of trading penny stocks. In fact, even the real experts still commit mistakes from time to time. Although committing a mistake is normal, doing the same mistake all over again is wrong. Always learn from your mistakes. Make sure you learn them. Also, do not beat yourself hard when you make a blunder. The important thing is that you learn. And by learning, you become a better trader.

Develop your strategy

Since the penny stocks market does not stop to move and change, you need to develop your strategy. A real strategy is a life-long journey. Your strategy must be flexible enough to adjust to the rapid changes in the market, and it must be effective enough to reap decent profits.

When to buy

There are two things about buying penny stocks: 1. which penny stocks to buy; and 2. the price. Ideally, you should make a buy order not simply when the price is low, but the important thing is that the price will experience a significant increase. To find out the best stocks to invest in takes a serious amount of research and study, time, and practice.

When to sell

This is the process of turning those profits into real cash. This is the way to enjoy your profits. It is suggested that even before you commence a trade (buy or sell), you should already know what to do with the stocks concerned. For example, say you have a target profit of 30%. Once your penny stocks increase their value and reach the said target percentage, you should immediately make a sell order. This advice is strongly recommended, especially for beginners. It is worth noting that many traders who lose their investment do not just lose their money because of picking the wrong stocks. In fact, they lose their money because they pick the right stocks but hold on to them for too long — so long that the value of the stocks drops significantly. Again, do not underestimate the high volatility of the penny stock market.

Of course, if circumstances strongly show that it would be a better decision not to make a sell order, then this is something that you should consider. To come up with a good decision, you need to update your research. Of course, the chance of earning bigger always comes with a risk. This option is not advisable for beginners. Beginners should aim for small and regular profits.

Stock split

A stock split is a good sign. This is where the company splits its every share. Therefore, each share will become two shares. For example, if you have 100 shares, a stock split will turn your shares into 200. Of course, the price will also be split. Example: if each penny share is priced at $1, the value will just be $0.50.

A stock split is a good sign. In fact, it is a good strategy to make a buy in immediately when a company declares a stock split. This is because a stock split usually means that the business is doing well. It is resorted to when the shares of the company have already achieved a significant increase in value that it has to split its stocks to come up with more shares that have a lower value. Most of the time, and if the company is able to maintain its excellent performance, the value of the new stocks also increase within a short period of time.

Beware of the reverse split

Unlike the stock split, the reverse split is a bad sign,

and you should stay away from it. Usually, companies resort to a reverse split when struggling to survive. As the name already implies, it is stock split in reverse. Example: Every 10 shares that you have will be considered a single share. Consequently, their values will also be added together. This is an attempt to make a company look like an attractive investment. Since the stocks are combined, it will appear to investors that the stocks of the company have increased in value significantly. Although, the truth is that the increase in price is not because of any legitimate flow of income, but the stocks are merely combined and manipulated to make them look like an attractive investment.

"Buy the rumor, sell the fact."

This is a common saying known to stock traders. One of the things that happen in the market is that when there is an upcoming big event, rumors spread easily and quickly. This draws so much attention in the penny stocks concerned, which usually result in an increase in their price. When traders see this, they make a buy order knowing that their price will increase dramatically. The obstacle here is that on the day of the event itself, instead of having a good increase in value, the price begins to drop — and it can be a big continuous drop.

Although this looks bad, it can also be profitable. What happens here is that the rumor makes the value increase so much way beyond the actual increase that the event can bring. But, as you can see, the price of the stocks concerned really increases. So, what you can do is to buy the stocks immediately while they are still low, and sell them right before the event or before their value drops.

Chapter 5:

Common Pitfalls and How to Avoid Them

There are pitfalls that beginners and even intermediate penny stock traders always fall for. The way to avoid these pitfalls is to be aware of them and to make the necessary adjustments in order to prevent them from happening.

Insufficient research

When it comes to trading penny stocks, research plays a very important role. This part is what differentiates trading penny stocks from gambling. Of course, if you do not exert the right amount of research, your decisions will be as good as relying on pure lack, which turns you into a gambler. Fundamental analysis is important if you want to increase your chances of earning a profit from a trade. Technical analysis or a study of graphs and charts are also helpful.

Just a hobby

If you want to approach trading penny stocks as a mere hobby and are not willing to make the necessary research, you would do better just by doing a demo play. Most of the time, those people who take this course a mere hobby only lose their money. To have continuous success trading penny stocks, you need to exert serious efforts, study, analysis, and practice.

Forcing a trade

Many investors make a trade simply because they see available funds in their account. Worse, they commence a trade even when surrounding circumstances do not show any promising outcome. Remember that when you trade, it is because there is a good potential to make money out of it. After all, you are not required to make any trade. So, if you do, make sure there is a good reason for it.

Inconsistent

Many traders fail to stick to their original strategy. Because of this, they could not tell whether or not such plan is good or not. Worse, they substitute a worse strategy in place of the original strategy. This usually happens when they see a sudden decrease in the value of their penny stocks. As much as practicable, you should stick to your plan so you will be able to measure just how effective it is. Of course, if the circumstances show that continuing with your strategy will only guarantee a loss of investment, then you can abandon your original strategy, but be sure to come up with a better one. This means that you will have to research again and test your next strategy.

Concentrating on good products

There is a difference between good products and right products. The right products that you should invest in are those whose value will increase. Good products do not always guarantee that the prices of stocks will also increase. After all, a business is not just made of good products. For a business to succeed, it also needs a strong and effective marketing plan, a reliable workforce, trustworthy suppliers, as well as a good public image, among others.

Pump and dump scheme

Pump and dump often happen. Even those who are aware of the pump and dump scheme still fall for it. The reason is because it is difficult to identify, especially if it is done by an "expert." This is another reason why you should develop your own understanding of the penny stock market and make your own decisions.

Short and distort scheme

This is also pump and dump but in reverse. This happens when a person borrows stocks and then sells them. After the sale, he spreads bad rumors about the stocks that he just sold. This will cause the value of those stocks to drop. When it drops, he then buys the stocks at a low price. In today's age where you can easily spread a message to the whole world with a click of a mouse, this scheme is as effective as the pump and dump. It has been used by hacks and fraudsters effectively.

Following expert advice

The problem here is that many "experts" often

oversell their expertise. In fact, you can find many "experts" who have more losses than profits. So, be very careful. Also, some of these "experts" operate a pump and dump scheme. It is good to be aware of expert advice, but it is more important that you learn to come up with your own decision. After all, even the real experts also experience bad trading days.

Greed

Greed is one thing that gamblers and traders usually have a problem with, which causes them to lose their money. Greed is deceiving because it appears reasonable. For example, why would you sell your penny stocks right after a 40% increase in value when you can expect it to grow even up to 100%? The thing is, many times, after the said 40% increase, it is followed by a big drop. The 100%, although possible, may never happen at all. This is why beginners you should stick to small and regular profits. You have to focus on increasing your rate of success. Continue to develop your strategy. After all, once you have an effective strategy with a high rate of success, you can always increase the amount of stocks that you trade.

Sticking to known strategies

The real experts study the known strategies and develop their own. After all, up to this time, there is no known strategy that can guarantee a profit. Although these known strategies can help lower your losses and increase the potential of making a profit, they do not guarantee a positive outcome. Also, the penny stock market continues to move and grow, it is only right that your strategy should also continuously develop and improve.

Investing more after a series of losses

Some people think that since they have lost several times in a row, the next trade will bring them a positive result. This is wrong. The penny stock market does not have a 50-50 probability, and the result of the next trade does not depend on the result of your previous trades. Every trade is unique and requires a separate research and analysis to succeed.

Wrong timing

When certain penny stocks gain popularity and their

price increase, some traders join the trend expecting to reap a high profit. The problem here is that right after a big increase in value, it can be followed by a significant decrease. Therefore, if you ride the trend too late, you will only lose your money.

Losing control

There are 3 ways to lose control: First is when you encounter a bad loss. It becomes tempting to chase after your losses. Second is when you get a good amount of profit. It becomes tempting to increase your target profit by investing more; and third, is when you barely gain or lose anything. Simply stated, every trade offers an opportunity for you to lose control and fail to stick to your plan. Having a journal will help you stick to your plan no matter what. Also, if you find it too tempting, just turn off your computer or mobile phone to prevent you from making a very risky trade.

Wrong understanding of volatility

Many traders think that volatility is something that balances itself in the long run. Meaning, after a big decrease in value, it will be followed by a massive increase after some time. Therefore, what they do is to place an investment right after a significant decrease in value of certain penny stocks. The problem here is that the volatility of penny stocks does not have a balanced nature. Even after a drop in price, it can still be followed by another dramatic decrease. In a positive light, a significant increase in value can still be followed by a continuous increase in value. Therefore, doing your research is very important. There are factors that affect the volatility and movement of penny stocks. If you analyze these factors, then you will be one step ahead.

Averaging down

Averaging down is when you buy particular stocks as their value decreases. This assures that you get to buy the stocks at a lower rate each time. This means that once their price finally increases, especially if more than the value at which you first bought it, all those stocks will make you give profits. Although this looks like a good strategy, this also means that you are in possession of a losing stock. If the said price increase does not happen, you will lose a lot of money. And, in the world of penny stocks, it is no surprise to see the price of a certain stock to continuously decrease uncontrollably. So, instead of averaging down and hoping for a positive outcome that may never happen, learn to identify the best penny stocks by doing a good amount of research and analysis of various businesses.

Conclusion

Thank for making it through to the end of this book, let's hope it was informative and able to provide you with all of the tools you need to achieve your goals whatever they may be.

The next step is to put everything into actual practice. So, open an account today with a trusted and reliable broker, begin trading, and rake in serious profits.

Finally, if you found this book useful in any way, a review on Amazon is always appreciated!

CPSIA information can be obtained
at www.ICGtesting.com
Printed in the USA
BVHW091057220221
600778BV00007B/711